Good day starts with gratitude

"Gratitude is the fairest blossom which springs from the soul."
Henry Ward Beecher

I'm thankful for: Date: -   -

- _____
- _____
- _____

I'm thankful for: Date: -   -

- _____
- _____
- _____

I'm thankful for: Date: -   -

- _____
- _____
- _____

I'm thankful for: Date: -   -

- _____
- _____
- _____

I'm thankful for: Date: -   -

- _____
- _____
- _____

I'm thankful for: Date: -   -

▪ _____

▪ _____

▪ _____

I'm thankful for: Date: -   -

▪ _____

▪ _____

▪ _____

I'm thankful for: Date: -   -

▪ _____

▪ _____

▪ _____

I'm thankful for: Date: -   -

▪ _____

▪ _____

▪ _____

I'm thankful for: Date: -   -

▪ _____

▪ _____

▪ _____

I'm thankful for: Date: -   -

▪ _____

▪ _____

▪ _____

I'm thankful for: Date: -   -

▪ _____

▪ _____

▪ _____

Good day starts with gratitude

"Gratitude turns what we have into enough."
Anonymous

I'm thankful for: Date: -   -
· _____
· _____
· _____

I'm thankful for: Date: -   -
· _____
· _____
· _____

I'm thankful for: Date: -   -
· _____
· _____
· _____

I'm thankful for: Date: -   -
· _____
· _____
· _____

I'm thankful for: Date: -   -
· _____
· _____
· _____

I'm thankful for:

Date: - -

- ....
- ....
- ....

I'm thankful for:

Date: - -

- ....
- ....
- ....

I'm thankful for:

Date: - -

- ....
- ....
- ....

I'm thankful for:

Date: - -

- ....
- ....
- ....

I'm thankful for:

Date: - -

- ....
- ....
- ....

I'm thankful for:

Date: - -

- ....
- ....
- ....

I'm thankful for:

Date: - -

- ....
- ....
- ....

Good day starts with gratitude

"Gratitude is a powerful catalyst for happiness. It's the spark that lights a fire of joy in your soul."
Amy Collette

I'm thankful for: Date: -   -

- _____
- _____
- _____

I'm thankful for: Date: -   -

- _____
- _____
- _____

I'm thankful for: Date: -   -

- _____
- _____
- _____

I'm thankful for: Date: -   -

- _____
- _____
- _____

I'm thankful for: Date: -   -

- _____
- _____
- _____

I'm thankful for: *Date:*   -   -

-
  ....
-
  ....
-
  ....

I'm thankful for: *Date:*   -   -

-
  ....
-
  ....
-
  ....

I'm thankful for: *Date:*   -   -

-
  ....
-
  ....
-
  ....

I'm thankful for: *Date:*   -   -

-
  ....
-
  ....
-
  ....

I'm thankful for: *Date:*   -   -

-
  ....
-
  ....
-
  ....

I'm thankful for: *Date:*   -   -

-
  ....
-
  ....
-
  ....

I'm thankful for: *Date:*   -   -

-
  ....
-
  ....
-
  ....

Good day starts with gratitude

"Gratitude makes sense of our past, brings peace for today, and creates a vision for tomorrow."
Melody Beattie

I'm thankful for: Date: -   -

▪ _____
▪ _____
▪ _____

I'm thankful for: Date: -   -

▪ _____
▪ _____
▪ _____

I'm thankful for: Date: -   -

▪ _____
▪ _____
▪ _____

I'm thankful for: Date: -   -

▪ _____
▪ _____
▪ _____

I'm thankful for: Date: -   -

▪ _____
▪ _____
▪ _____

I'm thankful for: *Date:*   -   -

* ....
* ....
* ....

I'm thankful for: *Date:*   -   -

* ....
* ....
* ....

I'm thankful for: *Date:*   -   -

* ....
* ....
* ....

I'm thankful for: *Date:*   -   -

* ....
* ....
* ....

I'm thankful for: *Date:*   -   -

* ....
* ....
* ....

I'm thankful for: *Date:*   -   -

* ....
* ....
* ....

I'm thankful for: *Date:*   -   -

* ....
* ....
* ....

Good day starts with gratitude

"Thankfulness is the beginning of gratitude. Gratitude is the completion of thankfulness. Thankfulness may consist merely of words. Gratitude is shown in acts."
Henri Frederic Amiel

I'm thankful for: Date: -   -

❋ _____
❋ _____
❋ _____

I'm thankful for: Date: -   -

❋ _____
❋ _____
❋ _____

I'm thankful for: Date: -   -

❋ _____
❋ _____
❋ _____

I'm thankful for: Date: -   -

❋ _____
❋ _____
❋ _____

I'm thankful for: Date: -   -

❋ _____
❋ _____
❋ _____

I'm thankful for: *Date:*   -   -

- ....
- ....
- ....

I'm thankful for: *Date:*   -   -

- ....
- ....
- ....

I'm thankful for: *Date:*   -   -

- ....
- ....
- ....

I'm thankful for: *Date:*   -   -

- ....
- ....
- ....

I'm thankful for: *Date:*   -   -

- ....
- ....
- ....

I'm thankful for: *Date:*   -   -

- ....
- ....
- ....

I'm thankful for: *Date:*   -   -

- ....
- ....
- ....

Good day starts with gratitude

"Happiness cannot be traveled to owned, earned, worn or consumed. Happiness is the spiritual experience of living every minute with love, grace, and gratitude."
Denis Waitley

I'm thankful for: Date: -   -

▪ _____

▪ _____

▪ _____

I'm thankful for: Date: -   -

▪ _____

▪ _____

▪ _____

I'm thankful for: Date: -   -

▪ _____

▪ _____

▪ _____

I'm thankful for: Date: -   -

▪ _____

▪ _____

▪ _____

I'm thankful for: Date: -   -

▪ _____

▪ _____

▪ _____

I'm thankful for: *Date:*   -   -

※ ....
_____

※ ....
_____

※ ....
_____

I'm thankful for: *Date:*   -   -

※ ....
_____

※ ....
_____

※
_____

I'm thankful for: *Date:*   -   -

※
_____

※ ....
_____

※ ....
_____

I'm thankful for: *Date:*   -   -

※ ....
_____

※ ....
_____

※ ....
_____

I'm thankful for: *Date:*   -   -

※ ....
_____

※ ....
_____

※
_____

I'm thankful for: *Date:*   -   -

※
_____

※
_____

※ ....
_____

I'm thankful for: *Date:*   -   -

※
_____

※ ....
_____

※ ....
_____

Good day starts with gratitude

"Joy is the simplest form of gratitude."
Karl Barth

I'm thankful for: Date: -   -
- ....
- ....
- ....

I'm thankful for: Date: -   -
- ....
- ....
- ....

I'm thankful for: Date: -   -
- ....
- ....
- ....

I'm thankful for: Date: -   -
- ....
- ....
- ....

I'm thankful for: Date: -   -
- ....
- ....
- ....

I'm thankful for: *Date:*   -   -

- _____
- _____
- _____

I'm thankful for: *Date:*   -   -

- _____
- _____
- _____

I'm thankful for: *Date:*   -   -

- _____
- _____
- _____

I'm thankful for: *Date:*   -   -

- _____
- _____
- _____

I'm thankful for: *Date:*   -   -

- _____
- _____
- _____

I'm thankful for: *Date:*   -   -

- _____
- _____
- _____

I'm thankful for: *Date:*   -   -

- _____
- _____
- _____

Good day starts with gratitude

"No one who achieves success does so without the help of others. The wise and confident acknowledge this help with gratitude."
Alfred North Whitehead

I'm thankful for: Date: -   -

※ _____
※ _____
※ _____

I'm thankful for: Date: -   -

※ _____
※ _____
※ _____

I'm thankful for: Date: -   -

※ _____
※ _____
※ _____

I'm thankful for: Date: -   -

※ _____
※ _____
※ _____

I'm thankful for: Date: -   -

※ _____
※ _____
※ _____

I'm thankful for:　　　　　　　　　　　　　　　　　Date:　-　-

* _____
* _____
* _____

I'm thankful for:　　　　　　　　　　　　　　　　　Date:　-　-

* _____
* _____
* _____

I'm thankful for:　　　　　　　　　　　　　　　　　Date:　-　-

* _____
* _____
* _____

I'm thankful for:　　　　　　　　　　　　　　　　　Date:　-　-

* _____
* _____
* _____

I'm thankful for:　　　　　　　　　　　　　　　　　Date:　-　-

* _____
* _____
* _____

I'm thankful for:　　　　　　　　　　　　　　　　　Date:　-　-

* _____
* _____
* _____

I'm thankful for:　　　　　　　　　　　　　　　　　Date:　-　-

* _____
* _____
* _____

Good day starts with gratitude

"In ordinary life, we hardly realize that we receive a great deal more than we give, and that it is only with gratitude that life becomes rich."
Dietrich Bonhoeffer

I'm thankful for: Date: -   -
※ _____
※ _____
※ _____

I'm thankful for: Date: -   -
※ _____
※ _____
※ _____

I'm thankful for: Date: -   -
※ _____
※ _____
※ _____

I'm thankful for: Date: -   -
※ _____
※ _____
※ _____

I'm thankful for: Date: -   -
※ _____
※ _____
※ _____

I'm thankful for: *Date:*   -   -

✳ ....
✳ ....
✳ ....

I'm thankful for: *Date:*   -   -

✳ ....
✳ ....
✳ _____

I'm thankful for: *Date:*   -   -

✳ _____
✳ ....
✳ ....

I'm thankful for: *Date:*   -   -

✳ _____
✳ ....
✳ ....

I'm thankful for: *Date:*   -   -

✳ _____
✳ ....
✳ _____

I'm thankful for: *Date:*   -   -

✳ _____
✳ _____
✳ ....

I'm thankful for: *Date:*   -   -

✳ _____
✳ ....
✳ ....

Good day starts with gratitude

"Gratitude is when memory is stored in the heart and not in the mind."
Lionel Hampton

I'm thankful for: Date: -   -
* _____
* _____
* _____

I'm thankful for: Date: -   -
* _____
* _____
* _____

I'm thankful for: Date: -   -
* _____
* _____
* _____

I'm thankful for: Date: -   -
* _____
* _____
* _____

I'm thankful for: Date: -   -
* _____
* _____
* _____

I'm thankful for: *Date:*   –   –

- _____
- _____
- _____

I'm thankful for: *Date:*   –   –

- _____
- _____
- _____

I'm thankful for: *Date:*   –   –

- _____
- _____
- _____

I'm thankful for: *Date:*   –   –

- _____
- _____
- _____

I'm thankful for: *Date:*   –   –

- _____
- _____
- _____

I'm thankful for: *Date:*   –   –

- _____
- _____
- _____

I'm thankful for: *Date:*   –   –

- _____
- _____
- _____

Good day starts with gratitude

"Gratitude is not only the greatest of virtues but the parent of all others."
Marcus Tullius Cicero

I'm thankful for: Date: -   -

- _____
- _____
- _____

I'm thankful for: Date: -   -

- _____
- _____
- _____

I'm thankful for: Date: -   -

- _____
- _____
- _____

I'm thankful for: Date: -   -

- _____
- _____
- _____

I'm thankful for: Date: -   -

- _____
- _____
- _____

I'm thankful for: *Date:*   -   -

※ ....
※ ....
※ ....

I'm thankful for: *Date:*   -   -

※ ....
※ ....
※ ....

I'm thankful for: *Date:*   -   -

※ ....
※ ....
※ ....

I'm thankful for: *Date:*   -   -

※ ....
※ ....
※ ....

I'm thankful for: *Date:*   -   -

※ ....
※ ....
※ ....

I'm thankful for: *Date:*   -   -

※ ....
※ ....
※ ....

I'm thankful for: *Date:*   -   -

※ ....
※ ....
※ ....

Good day starts with gratitude

"We often take for granted the very things that most deserve our gratitude."
Cynthia Ozick

I'm thankful for: Date: -   -
* _____
* _____
* _____

I'm thankful for: Date: -   -
* _____
* _____
* _____

I'm thankful for: Date: -   -
* _____
* _____
* _____

I'm thankful for: Date: -   -
* _____
* _____
* _____

I'm thankful for: Date: -   -
* _____
* _____
* _____

I'm thankful for: *Date:*   -   -

※ ....
※ ....
※ ....

I'm thankful for: *Date:*   -   -

※ ....
※ ....
※ ....

I'm thankful for: *Date:*   -   -

※ ....
※ ....
※ ....

I'm thankful for: *Date:*   -   -

※ ....
※ ....
※ ....

I'm thankful for: *Date:*   -   -

※ ....
※ ....
※ ....

I'm thankful for: *Date:*   -   -

※ ....
※ ....
※ ....

I'm thankful for: *Date:*   -   -

※ ....
※ ....
※ ....

Good day starts with gratitude

"You cannot do a kindness too soon because you never know how soon it will be too late."
Ralph Waldo Emerson

I'm thankful for: Date: -   -

- _____
- _____
- _____

I'm thankful for: Date: -   -

- _____
- _____
- _____

I'm thankful for: Date: -   -

- _____
- _____
- _____

I'm thankful for: Date: -   -

- _____
- _____
- _____

I'm thankful for: Date: -   -

- _____
- _____
- _____

I'm thankful for: *Date:*   -   -

- ▓
- ▓
- ▓

I'm thankful for: *Date:*   -   -

- ▓
- ▓
- ▓

I'm thankful for: *Date:*   -   -

- ▓
- ▓
- ▓

I'm thankful for: *Date:*   -   -

- ▓
- ▓
- ▓

I'm thankful for: *Date:*   -   -

- ▓
- ▓
- ▓

I'm thankful for: *Date:*   -   -

- ▓
- ▓
- ▓

I'm thankful for: *Date:*   -   -

- ▓
- ▓
- ▓

Good day starts with gratitude

"I would maintain that thanks are the highest form of thought, and that gratitude is happiness doubled by wonder."
Gilbert C. Chesterton

I'm thankful for: Date: -   -

※ _____
※ _____
※ _____

I'm thankful for: Date: -   -

※ _____
※ _____
※ _____

I'm thankful for: Date: -   -

※ _____
※ _____
※ _____

I'm thankful for: Date: -   -

※ _____
※ _____
※ _____

I'm thankful for: Date: -   -

※ _____
※ _____
※ _____

I'm thankful for: Date: -   -

-
-
-

I'm thankful for: Date: -   -

-
-
-

I'm thankful for: Date: -   -

-
-
-

I'm thankful for: Date: -   -

-
-
-

I'm thankful for: Date: -   -

-
-
-

I'm thankful for: Date: -   -

-
-
-

I'm thankful for: Date: -   -

-
-
-

Good day starts with gratitude

"Gratitude will shift you to a higher frequency, and you will attract much better things."
Rhonda Byrne

I'm thankful for: Date: -   -

-
-
-

I'm thankful for: Date: -   -

-
-
-

I'm thankful for: Date: -   -

-
-
-

I'm thankful for: Date: -   -

-
-
-

I'm thankful for: Date: -   -

-
-
-

I'm thankful for: *Date:*   -   -

-
-
-

I'm thankful for: *Date:*   -   -

-
-
-

I'm thankful for: *Date:*   -   -

-
-
-

I'm thankful for: *Date:*   -   -

-
-
-

I'm thankful for: *Date:*   -   -

-
-
-

I'm thankful for: *Date:*   -   -

-
-
-

I'm thankful for: *Date:*   -   -

-
-
-

Good day starts with gratitude

"When I started counting my blessings, my whole life turned around."
Willie Nelson

I'm thankful for: Date: -   -

- _____
- _____
- _____

I'm thankful for: Date: -   -

- _____
- _____
- _____

I'm thankful for: Date: -   -

- _____
- _____
- _____

I'm thankful for: Date: -   -

- _____
- _____
- _____

I'm thankful for: Date: -   -

- _____
- _____
- _____

I'm thankful for:

Date: - -

- _____
- _____
- _____

I'm thankful for:

Date: - -

- _____
- _____
- _____

I'm thankful for:

Date: - -

- _____
- _____
- _____

I'm thankful for:

Date: - -

- _____
- _____
- _____

I'm thankful for:

Date: - -

- _____
- _____
- _____

I'm thankful for:

Date: - -

- _____
- _____
- _____

I'm thankful for:

Date: - -

- _____
- _____
- _____

Good day starts with gratitude

"Let us rise up and be thankful, for if we didn't learn a lot today, at least we learned a little, and if we didn't learn a little, at least we didn't get sick, and if we got sick, at least we didn't die; so, let us all be thankful."

Buddha

I'm thankful for: Date: -   -

* _____
* _____
* _____

I'm thankful for: Date: -   -

* _____
* _____
* _____

I'm thankful for: Date: -   -

* _____
* _____
* _____

I'm thankful for: Date: -   -

* _____
* _____
* _____

I'm thankful for: Date: -   -

* _____
* _____
* _____

I'm thankful for:　　　　　　　　　　　　　　Date:　 -　 -

■　_____

■　_____

■　_____

I'm thankful for:　　　　　　　　　　　　　　Date:　 -　 -

■　_____

■　_____

■　_____

I'm thankful for:　　　　　　　　　　　　　　Date:　 -　 -

■　_____

■　_____

■　_____

I'm thankful for:　　　　　　　　　　　　　　Date:　 -　 -

■　_____

■　_____

■　_____

I'm thankful for:　　　　　　　　　　　　　　Date:　 -　 -

■　_____

■　_____

■　_____

I'm thankful for:　　　　　　　　　　　　　　Date:　 -　 -

■　_____

■　_____

■　_____

I'm thankful for:　　　　　　　　　　　　　　Date:　 -　 -

■　_____

■　_____

■　_____

Good day starts with gratitude

"Gratitude helps you to grow and expand; gratitude brings joy and laughter into your life and into the lives of all those around you."
Eileen Caddy

I'm thankful for: Date: -   -

* _____
* _____
* _____

I'm thankful for: Date: -   -

* _____
* _____
* _____

I'm thankful for: Date: -   -

* _____
* _____
* _____

I'm thankful for: Date: -   -

* _____
* _____
* _____

I'm thankful for: Date: -   -

* _____
* _____
* _____

I'm thankful for: *Date:*   -   -

- ....
- ....
-

I'm thankful for: *Date:*   -   -

- ....
- ....
-

I'm thankful for: *Date:*   -   -

-
-
-

I'm thankful for: *Date:*   -   -

-
- ....
-

I'm thankful for: *Date:*   -   -

-
-
-

I'm thankful for: *Date:*   -   -

-
-
- ....

I'm thankful for: *Date:*   -   -

- ....
- ....
- ....

Good day starts with gratitude

"Two kinds of gratitude: The sudden kind we feel for what we take; the larger kind we feel for what we give."
Edwin Arlington Robinson

I'm thankful for: Date: -   -

※ _____
※ _____
※ _____

I'm thankful for: Date: -   -

※ _____
※ _____
※ _____

I'm thankful for: Date: -   -

※ _____
※ _____
※ _____

I'm thankful for: Date: -   -

※ _____
※ _____
※ _____

I'm thankful for: Date: -   -

※ _____
※ _____
※ _____

I'm thankful for: *Date:*   -   -

I'm thankful for: *Date:*   -   -

I'm thankful for: *Date:*   -   -

I'm thankful for: *Date:*   -   -

I'm thankful for: *Date:*   -   -

I'm thankful for: *Date:*   -   -

I'm thankful for: *Date:*   -   -

Good day starts with gratitude

"Gratitude is the sweetest thing in a seekers life in all human life. If there is gratitude in your heart, then there will be tremendous sweetness in your eyes."
Sri Chinmoy

I'm thankful for: Date: -   -

❋ ....

❋ ....

❋ ....

I'm thankful for: Date: -   -

❋ ....

❋ ....

❋ ....

I'm thankful for: Date: -   -

❋ ....

❋ ....

❋ ....

I'm thankful for: Date: -   -

❋ ....

❋ ....

❋ ....

I'm thankful for: Date: -   -

❋ ....

❋ ....

❋ ....

I'm thankful for: *Date:*   -   -

❋ ....

❋ ....

❋ ....

I'm thankful for: *Date:*   -   -

❋ ....

❋ ....

❋ ....

I'm thankful for: *Date:*   -   -

❋ ....

❋ ....

❋ ....

I'm thankful for: *Date:*   -   -

❋ ....

❋ ....

❋ ....

I'm thankful for: *Date:*   -   -

❋ ....

❋ ....

❋ ....

I'm thankful for: *Date:*   -   -

❋ ....

❋ ....

❋ ....

I'm thankful for: *Date:*   -   -

❋ ....

❋ ....

❋ ....

Good day starts with gratitude

"As with all commandments, gratitude is a description of a successful mode of living. The thankful heart opens our eyes to a multitude of blessings that continually surround us."

James E. Faust

I'm thankful for: Date: -   -

❋ ....
❋ ....
❋ ....

I'm thankful for: Date: -   -

❋ ....
❋ ....
❋ ....

I'm thankful for: Date: -   -

❋ ....
❋ ....
❋ ....

I'm thankful for: Date: -   -

❋ ....
❋ ....
❋ ....

I'm thankful for: Date: -   -

❋ ....
❋ ....
❋ ....

I'm thankful for:

Date: - -

- ....
- ....
- ....

I'm thankful for:

Date: - -

- ....
- ....
- ....

I'm thankful for:

Date: - -

- ....
- ....
- ....

I'm thankful for:

Date: - -

- ....
- ....
- ....

I'm thankful for:

Date: - -

- ....
- ....
- ....

I'm thankful for:

Date: - -

- ....
- ....
- ....

I'm thankful for:

Date: - -

- ....
- ....
- ....

Good day starts with gratitude

"The more grateful I am, the more beauty I see."
Mary Davis

I'm thankful for: Date: -   -

I'm thankful for: Date: -   -

I'm thankful for: Date: -   -

I'm thankful for: Date: -   -

I'm thankful for: Date: -   -

I'm thankful for: *Date:*   -   -

░
⋯⋯⋯⋯⋯⋯⋯⋯⋯⋯⋯⋯⋯⋯⋯⋯⋯⋯⋯⋯⋯⋯⋯⋯⋯⋯⋯⋯⋯⋯⋯⋯⋯⋯
░
⋯⋯⋯⋯⋯⋯⋯⋯⋯⋯⋯⋯⋯⋯⋯⋯⋯⋯⋯⋯⋯⋯⋯⋯⋯⋯⋯⋯⋯⋯⋯⋯⋯⋯
░
⋯⋯⋯⋯⋯⋯⋯⋯⋯⋯⋯⋯⋯⋯⋯⋯⋯⋯⋯⋯⋯⋯⋯⋯⋯⋯⋯⋯⋯⋯⋯⋯⋯⋯

I'm thankful for: *Date:*   -   -

░
⋯⋯⋯⋯⋯⋯⋯⋯⋯⋯⋯⋯⋯⋯⋯⋯⋯⋯⋯⋯⋯⋯⋯⋯⋯⋯⋯⋯⋯⋯⋯⋯⋯⋯
░
⋯⋯⋯⋯⋯⋯⋯⋯⋯⋯⋯⋯⋯⋯⋯⋯⋯⋯⋯⋯⋯⋯⋯⋯⋯⋯⋯⋯⋯⋯⋯⋯⋯⋯
░
⋯⋯⋯⋯⋯⋯⋯⋯⋯⋯⋯⋯⋯⋯⋯⋯⋯⋯⋯⋯⋯⋯⋯⋯⋯⋯⋯⋯⋯⋯⋯⋯⋯⋯

I'm thankful for: *Date:*   -   -

░
⋯⋯⋯⋯⋯⋯⋯⋯⋯⋯⋯⋯⋯⋯⋯⋯⋯⋯⋯⋯⋯⋯⋯⋯⋯⋯⋯⋯⋯⋯⋯⋯⋯⋯
░
⋯⋯⋯⋯⋯⋯⋯⋯⋯⋯⋯⋯⋯⋯⋯⋯⋯⋯⋯⋯⋯⋯⋯⋯⋯⋯⋯⋯⋯⋯⋯⋯⋯⋯
░
⋯⋯⋯⋯⋯⋯⋯⋯⋯⋯⋯⋯⋯⋯⋯⋯⋯⋯⋯⋯⋯⋯⋯⋯⋯⋯⋯⋯⋯⋯⋯⋯⋯⋯

I'm thankful for: *Date:*   -   -

░
⋯⋯⋯⋯⋯⋯⋯⋯⋯⋯⋯⋯⋯⋯⋯⋯⋯⋯⋯⋯⋯⋯⋯⋯⋯⋯⋯⋯⋯⋯⋯⋯⋯⋯
░
⋯⋯⋯⋯⋯⋯⋯⋯⋯⋯⋯⋯⋯⋯⋯⋯⋯⋯⋯⋯⋯⋯⋯⋯⋯⋯⋯⋯⋯⋯⋯⋯⋯⋯
░
⋯⋯⋯⋯⋯⋯⋯⋯⋯⋯⋯⋯⋯⋯⋯⋯⋯⋯⋯⋯⋯⋯⋯⋯⋯⋯⋯⋯⋯⋯⋯⋯⋯⋯

I'm thankful for: *Date:*   -   -

░
⋯⋯⋯⋯⋯⋯⋯⋯⋯⋯⋯⋯⋯⋯⋯⋯⋯⋯⋯⋯⋯⋯⋯⋯⋯⋯⋯⋯⋯⋯⋯⋯⋯⋯
░
⋯⋯⋯⋯⋯⋯⋯⋯⋯⋯⋯⋯⋯⋯⋯⋯⋯⋯⋯⋯⋯⋯⋯⋯⋯⋯⋯⋯⋯⋯⋯⋯⋯⋯
░
⋯⋯⋯⋯⋯⋯⋯⋯⋯⋯⋯⋯⋯⋯⋯⋯⋯⋯⋯⋯⋯⋯⋯⋯⋯⋯⋯⋯⋯⋯⋯⋯⋯⋯

I'm thankful for: *Date:*   -   -

░
⋯⋯⋯⋯⋯⋯⋯⋯⋯⋯⋯⋯⋯⋯⋯⋯⋯⋯⋯⋯⋯⋯⋯⋯⋯⋯⋯⋯⋯⋯⋯⋯⋯⋯
░
⋯⋯⋯⋯⋯⋯⋯⋯⋯⋯⋯⋯⋯⋯⋯⋯⋯⋯⋯⋯⋯⋯⋯⋯⋯⋯⋯⋯⋯⋯⋯⋯⋯⋯
░
⋯⋯⋯⋯⋯⋯⋯⋯⋯⋯⋯⋯⋯⋯⋯⋯⋯⋯⋯⋯⋯⋯⋯⋯⋯⋯⋯⋯⋯⋯⋯⋯⋯⋯

I'm thankful for: *Date:*   -   -

░
⋯⋯⋯⋯⋯⋯⋯⋯⋯⋯⋯⋯⋯⋯⋯⋯⋯⋯⋯⋯⋯⋯⋯⋯⋯⋯⋯⋯⋯⋯⋯⋯⋯⋯
░
⋯⋯⋯⋯⋯⋯⋯⋯⋯⋯⋯⋯⋯⋯⋯⋯⋯⋯⋯⋯⋯⋯⋯⋯⋯⋯⋯⋯⋯⋯⋯⋯⋯⋯
░
⋯⋯⋯⋯⋯⋯⋯⋯⋯⋯⋯⋯⋯⋯⋯⋯⋯⋯⋯⋯⋯⋯⋯⋯⋯⋯⋯⋯⋯⋯⋯⋯⋯⋯

Good day starts with gratitude

"The deepest craving of human nature is the need to be appreciated."
William James

I'm thankful for: Date: -   -

※ _____

※ _____

※ _____

I'm thankful for: Date: -   -

※ _____

※ _____

※ _____

I'm thankful for: Date: -   -

※ _____

※ _____

※ _____

I'm thankful for: Date: -   -

※ _____

※ _____

※ _____

I'm thankful for: Date: -   -

※ _____

※ _____

※ _____

I'm thankful for: *Date:*   -   -

※ ....
....
※ ....
....
※ ....

I'm thankful for: *Date:*   -   -

※ ....
....
※ ....
....
※ ....

I'm thankful for: *Date:*   -   -

※ ....
....
※ ....
....
※ ....

I'm thankful for: *Date:*   -   -

※ ....
....
※ ....
....
※ ....

I'm thankful for: *Date:*   -   -

※ ....
....
※ ....
....
※ ....

I'm thankful for: *Date:*   -   -

※ ....
....
※ ....
....
※ ....

I'm thankful for: *Date:*   -   -

※ ....
....
※ ....
....
※ ....

Good day starts with gratitude

"There is a calmness to a life lived in gratitude, a quiet joy."
Ralph H. Blum

I'm thankful for: Date: -   -

※ _____
※ _____
※ _____

I'm thankful for: Date: -   -

※ _____
※ _____
※ _____

I'm thankful for: Date: -   -

※ _____
※ _____
※ _____

I'm thankful for: Date: -   -

※ _____
※ _____
※ _____

I'm thankful for: Date: -   -

※ _____
※ _____
※ _____

I'm thankful for:

Date: - -

■ _____

■ _____

■ _____

I'm thankful for:

Date: - -

■ _____

■ _____

■ _____

I'm thankful for:

Date: - -

■ _____

■ _____

■ _____

I'm thankful for:

Date: - -

■ _____

■ _____

■ _____

I'm thankful for:

Date: - -

■ _____

■ _____

■ _____

I'm thankful for:

Date: - -

■ _____

■ _____

■ _____

I'm thankful for:

Date: - -

■ _____

■ _____

■ _____

Good day starts with gratitude

"Gratitude is the most exquisite form of courtesy."
Jacques Maritain

I'm thankful for: Date: - -

- _____
- _____
- _____

I'm thankful for: Date: - -

- _____
- _____
- _____

I'm thankful for: Date: - -

- _____
- _____
- _____

I'm thankful for: Date: - -

- _____
- _____
- _____

I'm thankful for: Date: - -

- _____
- _____
- _____

I'm thankful for: *Date:*   -   -

- ....
- ....
- ....

I'm thankful for: *Date:*   -   -

- ....
- ....
- ....

I'm thankful for: *Date:*   -   -

- ....
- ....
- ....

I'm thankful for: *Date:*   -   -

- ....
- ....
- ....

I'm thankful for: *Date:*   -   -

- ....
- ....
- ....

I'm thankful for: *Date:*   -   -

- ....
- ....
- ....

I'm thankful for: *Date:*   -   -

- ....
- ....
- ....

Good day starts with gratitude

"The root of joy is gratefulness."
David Steindl-Rast

I'm thankful for: Date: -   -

- _____
- _____
- _____

I'm thankful for: Date: -   -

- _____
- _____
- _____

I'm thankful for: Date: -   -

- _____
- _____
- _____

I'm thankful for: Date: -   -

- _____
- _____
- _____

I'm thankful for: Date: -   -

- _____
- _____
- _____

I'm thankful for: Date: -   -

-
-
-

I'm thankful for: Date: -   -

-
-
-

I'm thankful for: Date: -   -

-
-
-

I'm thankful for: Date: -   -

-
-
-

I'm thankful for: Date: -   -

-
-
-

I'm thankful for: Date: -   -

-
-
-

I'm thankful for: Date: -   -

-
-
-

Good day starts with gratitude

"I've had a remarkable life. I seem to be in such good places at the right time. You know, if you were to ask me to sum my life up in one word, gratitude."
Dietrich Bonhoeffer

I'm thankful for: Date: -   -

- _____
- _____
- _____

I'm thankful for: Date: -   -

- _____
- _____
- _____

I'm thankful for: Date: -   -

- _____
- _____
- _____

I'm thankful for: Date: -   -

- _____
- _____
- _____

I'm thankful for: Date: -   -

- _____
- _____
- _____

I'm thankful for:　　　　　　　　　　　　　　　　　　*Date:*　　–　　–

- _____
- _____
- _____

I'm thankful for:　　　　　　　　　　　　　　　　　　*Date:*　　–　　–

- _____
- _____
- _____

I'm thankful for:　　　　　　　　　　　　　　　　　　*Date:*　　–　　–

- _____
- _____
- _____

I'm thankful for:　　　　　　　　　　　　　　　　　　*Date:*　　–　　–

- _____
- _____
- _____

I'm thankful for:　　　　　　　　　　　　　　　　　　*Date:*　　–　　–

- _____
- _____
- _____

I'm thankful for:　　　　　　　　　　　　　　　　　　*Date:*　　–　　–

- _____
- _____
- _____

I'm thankful for:　　　　　　　　　　　　　　　　　　*Date:*　　–　　–

- _____
- _____
- _____

Good day starts with gratitude

"He is a wise man who does not grieve for the things which he has not, but rejoices for those which he has."
Epictetus

I'm thankful for: Date: -   -
- _____
- _____
- _____

I'm thankful for: Date: -   -
- _____
- _____
- _____

I'm thankful for: Date: -   -
- _____
- _____
- _____

I'm thankful for: Date: -   -
- _____
- _____
- _____

I'm thankful for: Date: -   -
- _____
- _____
- _____

I'm thankful for: *Date:*   -   -

- ....
- _____
- ....

I'm thankful for: *Date:*   -   -

- _____
- _____
- _____

I'm thankful for: *Date:*   -   -

- _____
- ....
- _____

I'm thankful for: *Date:*   -   -

- _____
- ....
- _____

I'm thankful for: *Date:*   -   -

- _____
- _____
- _____

I'm thankful for: *Date:*   -   -

- _____
- _____
- ....

I'm thankful for: *Date:*   -   -

- _____
- ....
- ....

Good day starts with gratitude

"Gratitude unlocks the fullness of life. It turns what we have into enough, and more. It turns denial into acceptance, chaos to order, confusion to clarity. It can turn a meal into a feast, a house into a home, a stranger into a friend.
Melody Beattie

I'm thankful for: Date: -   -

_____

_____

_____

I'm thankful for: Date: -   -

_____

_____

_____

I'm thankful for: Date: -   -

_____

_____

_____

I'm thankful for: Date: -   -

_____

_____

_____

I'm thankful for: Date: -   -

_____

_____

_____

I'm thankful for: *Date:*   -   -

- _____
- _____
- _____

I'm thankful for: *Date:*   -   -

- _____
- _____
- _____

I'm thankful for: *Date:*   -   -

- _____
- _____
- _____

I'm thankful for: *Date:*   -   -

- _____
- _____
- _____

I'm thankful for: *Date:*   -   -

- _____
- _____
- _____

I'm thankful for: *Date:*   -   -

- _____
- _____
- _____

I'm thankful for: *Date:*   -   -

- _____
- _____
- _____

Good day starts with gratitude

"Being thankful is not always experienced as a natural state of existence, we must work at it, akin to a type of strength training for the heart."
Larissa Gomez

I'm thankful for: Date: -   -

▪ _____
▪ _____
▪ _____

I'm thankful for: Date: -   -

▪ _____
▪ _____
▪ _____

I'm thankful for: Date: -   -

▪ _____
▪ _____
▪ _____

I'm thankful for: Date: -   -

▪ _____
▪ _____
▪ _____

I'm thankful for: Date: -   -

▪ _____
▪ _____
▪ _____

I'm thankful for: *Date:*   -   -

- _____
- _____
- _____

I'm thankful for: *Date:*   -   -

- _____
- _____
- _____

I'm thankful for: *Date:*   -   -

- _____
- _____
- _____

I'm thankful for: *Date:*   -   -

- _____
- _____
- _____

I'm thankful for: *Date:*   -   -

- _____
- _____
- _____

I'm thankful for: *Date:*   -   -

- _____
- _____
- _____

I'm thankful for: *Date:*   -   -

- _____
- _____
- _____

Good day starts with gratitude

"Today I choose to live with gratitude for the love that fills my heart, the peace that rests within my spirit, and the voice of hope that says all things are possible."
Anonymous

I'm thankful for: Date: -   -
- _____
- _____
- _____

I'm thankful for: Date: -   -
- _____
- _____
- _____

I'm thankful for: Date: -   -
- _____
- _____
- _____

I'm thankful for: Date: -   -
- _____
- _____
- _____

I'm thankful for: Date: -   -
- _____
- _____
- _____

I'm thankful for: *Date:*   –   –

- _____
- _____
- _____

I'm thankful for: *Date:*   –   –

- _____
- _____
- _____

I'm thankful for: *Date:*   –   –

- _____
- _____
- _____

I'm thankful for: *Date:*   –   –

- _____
- _____
- _____

I'm thankful for: *Date:*   –   –

- _____
- _____
- _____

I'm thankful for: *Date:*   –   –

- _____
- _____
- _____

I'm thankful for: *Date:*   –   –

- _____
- _____
- _____

Good day starts with gratitude

"We can only be said to be alive in those moments when our hearts are conscious of our treasures."
Thornton Wilder

I'm thankful for: Date: -   -
- ....
- ....
- ....

I'm thankful for: Date: -   -
- ....
- ....
- ....

I'm thankful for: Date: -   -
- ....
- ....
- ....

I'm thankful for: Date: -   -
- ....
- ....
- ....

I'm thankful for: Date: -   -
- ....
- ....
- ....

I'm thankful for: *Date:* - -

-
-
-

I'm thankful for: *Date:* - -

-
-
-

I'm thankful for: *Date:* - -

-
-
-

I'm thankful for: *Date:* - -

-
-
-

I'm thankful for: *Date:* - -

-
-
-

I'm thankful for: *Date:* - -

-
-
-

I'm thankful for: *Date:* - -

-
-
-

Good day starts with gratitude

"If you concentrate on finding whatever is good in every situation, you will discover that your life will suddenly be filled with gratitude, a feeling that nurtures the soul."
Rabbi Harold Kushner

I'm thankful for: Date: -   -
- _____
- _____
- _____

I'm thankful for: Date: -   -
- _____
- _____
- _____

I'm thankful for: Date: -   -
- _____
- _____
- _____

I'm thankful for: Date: -   -
- _____
- _____
- _____

I'm thankful for: Date: -   -
- _____
- _____
- _____

I'm thankful for: *Date:*   -   -

-
-
-

I'm thankful for: *Date:*   -   -

-
-
-

I'm thankful for: *Date:*   -   -

-
-
-

I'm thankful for: *Date:*   -   -

-
-
-

I'm thankful for: *Date:*   -   -

-
-
-

I'm thankful for: *Date:*   -   -

-
-
-

I'm thankful for: *Date:*   -   -

-
-
-

Good day starts with gratitude

"Be thankful for what you have; you'll end up having more. If you concentrate on what you don't have, you will never, ever have enough."
Oprah Winfrey

I'm thankful for: Date: -   -
- _____
- _____
- _____

I'm thankful for: Date: -   -
- _____
- _____
- _____

I'm thankful for: Date: -   -
- _____
- _____
- _____

I'm thankful for: Date: -   -
- _____
- _____
- _____

I'm thankful for: Date: -   -
- _____
- _____
- _____

I'm thankful for: *Date:*   -   -

- ....
- ....
- ....

I'm thankful for: *Date:*   -   -

- ....
- ....
- ....

I'm thankful for: *Date:*   -   -

- ....
- ....
- ....

I'm thankful for: *Date:*   -   -

- ....
- ....
- ....

I'm thankful for: *Date:*   -   -

- ....
- ....
- ....

I'm thankful for: *Date:*   -   -

- ....
- ....
- ....

I'm thankful for: *Date:*   -   -

- ....
- ....
- ....

Good day starts with gratitude

"As we express our gratitude, we must never forget that the highest appreciation is not to utter words, but to live by them."
John F. Kennedy

I'm thankful for: Date: -   -
- _____
- _____
- _____

I'm thankful for: Date: -   -
- _____
- _____
- _____

I'm thankful for: Date: -   -
- _____
- _____
- _____

I'm thankful for: Date: -   -
- _____
- _____
- _____

I'm thankful for: Date: -   -
- _____
- _____
- _____

I'm thankful for: *Date:*   -   -

- ....
- ....
- ....

I'm thankful for: *Date:*   -   -

- ....
- ....
- ....

I'm thankful for: *Date:*   -   -

- ....
- ....
- ....

I'm thankful for: *Date:*   -   -

- ....
- ....
- ....

I'm thankful for: *Date:*   -   -

- ....
- ....
- ....

I'm thankful for: *Date:*   -   -

- ....
- ....
- ....

I'm thankful for: *Date:*   -   -

- ....
- ....
- ....

Good day starts with gratitude

"I looked around and thought about my life. I felt grateful. I noticed every detail.
That is the key to time travel. You can only move if you are actually in the moment.
You have to be where you are to get where you need to go."
Amy Poehler

I'm thankful for: Date: -   -
- _____
- _____
- _____

I'm thankful for: Date: -   -
- _____
- _____
- _____

I'm thankful for: Date: -   -
- _____
- _____
- _____

I'm thankful for: Date: -   -
- _____
- _____
- _____

I'm thankful for: Date: -   -
- _____
- _____
- _____

I'm thankful for: *Date:*   -   -

- _____
- _____
- _____

I'm thankful for: *Date:*   -   -

- _____
- _____
- _____

I'm thankful for: *Date:*   -   -

- _____
- _____
- _____

I'm thankful for: *Date:*   -   -

- _____
- _____
- _____

I'm thankful for: *Date:*   -   -

- _____
- _____
- _____

I'm thankful for: *Date:*   -   -

- _____
- _____
- _____

I'm thankful for: *Date:*   -   -

- _____
- _____
- _____

Good day starts with gratitude

"Gratitude for the present moment and the fullness of life now is the true prosperity."
Eckhart Tolle

I'm thankful for: Date: -   -
- _____
- _____
- _____

I'm thankful for: Date: -   -
- _____
- _____
- _____

I'm thankful for: Date: -   -
- _____
- _____
- _____

I'm thankful for: Date: -   -
- _____
- _____
- _____

I'm thankful for: Date: -   -
- _____
- _____
- _____

I'm thankful for: *Date:*   –   –

- _____
- _____
- _____

I'm thankful for: *Date:*   –   –

- _____
- _____
- _____

I'm thankful for: *Date:*   –   –

- _____
- _____
- _____

I'm thankful for: *Date:*   –   –

- _____
- _____
- _____

I'm thankful for: *Date:*   –   –

- _____
- _____
- _____

I'm thankful for: *Date:*   –   –

- _____
- _____
- _____

I'm thankful for: *Date:*   –   –

- _____
- _____
- _____

Good day starts with gratitude

"Gratitude is the sign of noble souls."
Aesop

I'm thankful for: Date: -   -

- _____
- _____
- _____

I'm thankful for: Date: -   -

- _____
- _____
- _____

I'm thankful for: Date: -   -

- _____
- _____
- _____

I'm thankful for: Date: -   -

- _____
- _____
- _____

I'm thankful for: Date: -   -

- _____
- _____
- _____

I'm thankful for: *Date:*   -   -

-
-
-

I'm thankful for: *Date:*   -   -

-
-
-

I'm thankful for: *Date:*   -   -

-
-
-

I'm thankful for: *Date:*   -   -

-
-
-

I'm thankful for: *Date:*   -   -

-
-
-

I'm thankful for: *Date:*   -   -

-
-
-

I'm thankful for: *Date:*   -   -

-
-
-

Good day starts with gratitude

"Feeling gratitude and not expressing it is like wrapping a present and not giving it."
William Arthur Ward

I'm thankful for: Date: -   -

- _____
- _____
- _____

I'm thankful for: Date: -   -

- _____
- _____
- _____

I'm thankful for: Date: -   -

- _____
- _____
- _____

I'm thankful for: Date: -   -

- _____
- _____
- _____

I'm thankful for: Date: -   -

- _____
- _____
- _____

I'm thankful for: *Date:*   -   -

-
-
-

I'm thankful for: *Date:*   -   -

-
-
-

I'm thankful for: *Date:*   -   -

-
-
-

I'm thankful for: *Date:*   -   -

-
-
-

I'm thankful for: *Date:*   -   -

-
-
-

I'm thankful for: *Date:*   -   -

-
-
-

I'm thankful for: *Date:*   -   -

-
-
-

Good day starts with gratitude

"Develop an attitude of gratitude, and give thanks for everything that happens to you, knowing that every step forward is a step toward achieving something bigger and better than your current situation."
Brian Tracy

I'm thankful for: Date: -   -

- _____
- _____
- _____

I'm thankful for: Date: -   -

- _____
- _____
- _____

I'm thankful for: Date: -   -

- _____
- _____
- _____

I'm thankful for: Date: -   -

- _____
- _____
- _____

I'm thankful for: Date: -   -

- _____
- _____
- _____

I'm thankful for: *Date:*   -   -

- ▓ ....
- ▓ ....
- ▓ ....

I'm thankful for: *Date:*   -   -

- ▓ ....
- ▓ ....
- ▓ ....

I'm thankful for: *Date:*   -   -

- ▓ ....
- ▓ ....
- ▓ ....

I'm thankful for: *Date:*   -   -

- ▓ ....
- ▓ ....
- ▓ ....

I'm thankful for: *Date:*   -   -

- ▓ ....
- ▓ ....
- ▓ ....

I'm thankful for: *Date:*   -   -

- ▓ ....
- ▓ ....
- ▓ ....

I'm thankful for: *Date:*   -   -

- ▓ ....
- ▓ ....
- ▓ ....

Good day starts with gratitude

"Opening your eyes to more of the world around you can deeply enhance your gratitude practice."
Derrick Carpenter

I'm thankful for: Date: -   -

- _____
- _____
- _____

I'm thankful for: Date: -   -

- _____
- _____
- _____

I'm thankful for: Date: -   -

- _____
- _____
- _____

I'm thankful for: Date: -   -

- _____
- _____
- _____

I'm thankful for: Date: -   -

- _____
- _____
- _____

I'm thankful for: Date: -   -

- _____
- _____
- _____

I'm thankful for: Date: -   -

- _____
- _____
- _____

I'm thankful for: Date: -   -

- _____
- _____
- _____

I'm thankful for: Date: -   -

- _____
- _____
- _____

I'm thankful for: Date: -   -

- _____
- _____
- _____

I'm thankful for: Date: -   -

- _____
- _____
- _____

I'm thankful for: Date: -   -

- _____
- _____
- _____

Good day starts with gratitude

"Nothing is more honorable than a grateful heart."
Lucius Annaeus Seneca

I'm thankful for: Date: -   -
- _____
- _____
- _____

I'm thankful for: Date: -   -
- _____
- _____
- _____

I'm thankful for: Date: -   -
- _____
- _____
- _____

I'm thankful for: Date: -   -
- _____
- _____
- _____

I'm thankful for: Date: -   -
- _____
- _____
- _____

I'm thankful for: Date: -   -

-
-
-

I'm thankful for: Date: -   -

-
-
-

I'm thankful for: Date: -   -

-
-
-

I'm thankful for: Date: -   -

-
-
-

I'm thankful for: Date: -   -

-
-
-

I'm thankful for: Date: -   -

-
-
-

I'm thankful for: Date: -   -

-
-
-

Good day starts with gratitude

"Be grateful for what you already have while you pursue your goals. If you aren't grateful for what you already have, what makes you think you would be happy with more."

Roy T. Bennett

I'm thankful for: Date: -   -

- _____
- _____
- _____

I'm thankful for: Date: -   -

- _____
- _____
- _____

I'm thankful for: Date: -   -

- _____
- _____
- _____

I'm thankful for: Date: -   -

- _____
- _____
- _____

I'm thankful for: Date: -   -

- _____
- _____
- _____

I'm thankful for: *Date:*   -   -

- ....
- ....
- ....

I'm thankful for: *Date:*   -   -

- ....
- ....
- ....

I'm thankful for: *Date:*   -   -

- ....
- ....
- ....

I'm thankful for: *Date:*   -   -

- ....
- ....
- ....

I'm thankful for: *Date:*   -   -

- ....
- ....
- ....

I'm thankful for: *Date:*   -   -

- ....
- ....
- ....

I'm thankful for: *Date:*   -   -

- ....
- ....
- ....

Good day starts with gratitude

"Train yourself never to put off the word or action for the expression of gratitude."
Albert Schweitzer

I'm thankful for: Date: -   -
- _____
- _____
- _____

I'm thankful for: Date: -   -
- _____
- _____
- _____

I'm thankful for: Date: -   -
- _____
- _____
- _____

I'm thankful for: Date: -   -
- _____
- _____
- _____

I'm thankful for: Date: -   -
- _____
- _____
- _____

I'm thankful for: *Date:*   -   -

- ....
- ....
- ....

I'm thankful for: *Date:*   -   -

- ....
- ....
- ....

I'm thankful for: *Date:*   -   -

- ....
- ....
- ....

I'm thankful for: *Date:*   -   -

- ....
- ....
- ....

I'm thankful for: *Date:*   -   -

- ....
- ....
- ....

I'm thankful for: *Date:*   -   -

- ....
- ....
- ....

I'm thankful for: *Date:*   -   -

- ....
- ....
- ....

Good day starts with gratitude

"Gratitude is riches. Complaint is poverty."
Doris Day

I'm thankful for: Date: -   -

- _____
- _____
- _____

I'm thankful for: Date: -   -

- _____
- _____
- _____

I'm thankful for: Date: -   -

- _____
- _____
- _____

I'm thankful for: Date: -   -

- _____
- _____
- _____

I'm thankful for: Date: -   -

- _____
- _____
- _____

I'm thankful for: *Date:*   -   -

- _____
- _____
- _____

I'm thankful for: *Date:*   -   -

- _____
- _____
- _____

I'm thankful for: *Date:*   -   -

- _____
- _____
- _____

I'm thankful for: *Date:*   -   -

- _____
- _____
- _____

I'm thankful for: *Date:*   -   -

- _____
- _____
- _____

I'm thankful for: *Date:*   -   -

- _____
- _____
- _____

I'm thankful for: *Date:*   -   -

- _____
- _____
- _____

Good day starts with gratitude

"Gratitude is an antidote to negative emotions, a neutralizer of envy, hostility, worry, and irritation. It is savoring; it is not taking things for granted; it is present-oriented."
Sonja Lyubomirsky

I'm thankful for: Date: -   -
- _____
- _____
- _____

I'm thankful for: Date: -   -
- _____
- _____
- _____

I'm thankful for: Date: -   -
- _____
- _____
- _____

I'm thankful for: Date: -   -
- _____
- _____
- _____

I'm thankful for: Date: -   -
- _____
- _____
- _____

I'm thankful for: *Date:*   -   -

-
-
-

I'm thankful for: *Date:*   -   -

-
-
-

I'm thankful for: *Date:*   -   -

-
-
-

I'm thankful for: *Date:*   -   -

-
-
-

I'm thankful for: *Date:*   -   -

-
-
-

I'm thankful for: *Date:*   -   -

-
-
-

I'm thankful for: *Date:*   -   -

-
-
-

Good day starts with gratitude

"When you are grateful, fear disappears and abundance appears."
Anthony Robbins

I'm thankful for: Date: -   -

▓ _____

▓ _____

▓ _____

I'm thankful for: Date: -   -

▓ _____

▓ _____

▓ _____

I'm thankful for: Date: -   -

▓ _____

▓ _____

▓ _____

I'm thankful for: Date: -   -

▓ _____

▓ _____

▓ _____

I'm thankful for: Date: -   -

▓ _____

▓ _____

▓ _____

I'm thankful for: *Date:*   -   -

- _____
- _____
- _____

I'm thankful for: *Date:*   -   -

- _____
- _____
- _____

I'm thankful for: *Date:*   -   -

- _____
- _____
- _____

I'm thankful for: *Date:*   -   -

- _____
- _____
- _____

I'm thankful for: *Date:*   -   -

- _____
- _____
- _____

I'm thankful for: *Date:*   -   -

- _____
- _____
- _____

I'm thankful for: *Date:*   -   -

- _____
- _____
- _____

Good day starts with gratitude

"What separates privilege from entitlement is gratitude."
Brene Brown

I'm thankful for: Date: -   -

▪ _____
▪ _____
▪ _____

I'm thankful for: Date: -   -

▪ _____
▪ _____
▪ _____

I'm thankful for: Date: -   -

▪ _____
▪ _____
▪ _____

I'm thankful for: Date: -   -

▪ _____
▪ _____
▪ _____

I'm thankful for: Date: -   -

▪ _____
▪ _____
▪ _____

I'm thankful for: *Date:*   -   -
- ....
- ....
- ....

I'm thankful for: *Date:*   -   -
- ....
- ....
- ....

I'm thankful for: *Date:*   -   -
- ....
- ....
- ....

I'm thankful for: *Date:*   -   -
- ....
- ....
- ....

I'm thankful for: *Date:*   -   -
- ....
- ....
- ....

I'm thankful for: *Date:*   -   -
- ....
- ....
- ....

I'm thankful for: *Date:*   -   -
- ....
- ....
- ....

Good day starts with gratitude

"When it comes to life the critical thing is whether you take things for granted or take them with gratitude."
G.K. Chesterton

I'm thankful for: Date: -   -

- _____
- _____
- _____

I'm thankful for: Date: -   -

- _____
- _____
- _____

I'm thankful for: Date: -   -

- _____
- _____
- _____

I'm thankful for: Date: -   -

- _____
- _____
- _____

I'm thankful for: Date: -   -

- _____
- _____
- _____

I'm thankful for: *Date:*   -   -
- ....
- ....
- ....

I'm thankful for: *Date:*   -   -
- ....
- ....
- ....

I'm thankful for: *Date:*   -   -
- ....
- ....
- ....

I'm thankful for: *Date:*   -   -
- ....
- ....
- ....

I'm thankful for: *Date:*   -   -
- ....
- ....
- ....

I'm thankful for: *Date:*   -   -
- ....
- ....
- ....

I'm thankful for: *Date:*   -   -
- ....
- ....
- ....

Good day starts with gratitude

"The way to develop the best that is in a person is by appreciation and encouragement."
Charles Schwab

I'm thankful for: Date: -   -

_____
_____
_____

I'm thankful for: Date: -   -

_____
_____
_____

I'm thankful for: Date: -   -

_____
_____
_____

I'm thankful for: Date: -   -

_____
_____
_____

I'm thankful for: Date: -   -

_____
_____
_____

I'm thankful for:

Date: - -

- _____
- _____
- _____

I'm thankful for:

Date: - -

- _____
- _____
- _____

I'm thankful for:

Date: - -

- _____
- _____
- _____

I'm thankful for:

Date: - -

- _____
- _____
- _____

I'm thankful for:

Date: - -

- _____
- _____
- _____

I'm thankful for:

Date: - -

- _____
- _____
- _____

I'm thankful for:

Date: - -

- _____
- _____
- _____

Good day starts with gratitude

.

"Enjoy the little things, for one day you may look back and realize they were the big things."
Robert Brault

I'm thankful for: Date: -   -

- _____
- _____
- _____

I'm thankful for: Date: -   -

- _____
- _____
- _____

I'm thankful for: Date: -   -

- _____
- _____
- _____

I'm thankful for: Date: -   -

- _____
- _____
- _____

I'm thankful for: Date: -   -

- _____
- _____
- _____

I'm thankful for: *Date:*   -   -

-
-
-

I'm thankful for: *Date:*   -   -

-
-
-

I'm thankful for: *Date:*   -   -

-
-
-

I'm thankful for: *Date:*   -   -

-
-
-

I'm thankful for: *Date:*   -   -

-
-
-

I'm thankful for: *Date:*   -   -

-
-
-

I'm thankful for: *Date:*   -   -

-
-
-

Your life is as Good as your Mindset

Printed in Great Britain
by Amazon